How to use this book

Follow the advice, in italics, given for you on each page.
Support the children as they read the text that is shaded in cream.
***Praise** the children at every step!*
Detailed guidance is provided in the Read Write Inc. Phonics Handbook.

9 reading activities
Children:
1   *Practise reading the speed sounds.*
2   *Read the green, red and challenge words for the non-fiction text.*
3   *Listen as you read the introduction.*
4   *Discuss the vocabulary check with you.*
5   *Read the non-fiction text.*
6   *Re-read the non-fiction text and discuss the 'questions to talk about'.*
7   *Re-read the non-fiction text with fluency and expression.*
8   *Answer the questions to 'read and answer'.*
9   *Practise reading the speed words.*

Speed sounds

Consonants Say the pure sounds (do not add 'uh').

f ff	l ll le	m mm	n nn kn	r rr wr	s ss	v ve	z zz s	sh	th	ng nk

b bb	c k (ck)	d dd	g gg	h	j	p pp	qu	t tt	w wh	x	y	ch tch

Vowels Say the vowel sound and then the word, eg 'a', 'at'.

at	hen head	in	on	up	day make	see tea happy he	high smile lie find	blow home no

zoo	look	car	for door snore	fair	whirl	shout	boy spoil

*Each box contains one sound but sometimes more than one grapheme. Focus graphemes are **circled**.*

Green words

Read in Fred Talk (pure sounds).

peach	read	cheap	real	feast	heap	cream	clean
seat	eat	see	need	sweet	make	cake	flake
take	base	first	bowl	with	adult	chunk	

Read in syllables.

part`y → party    eas`y → easy   car`ton → carton

dair`y → dairy    foll`ow → follow   fin`ish → finish

bir th`day → birthday   cho'co'late → chocolate

Read the root word first and then with the ending.

treat → treats   grape → grapes   scoop → scoops

stick → sticking   cut → cutting

Red words

you your some the by

Challenge words

custard

How to make a peach treat

Introduction

In this book you will find out how to make a sweet dessert with peaches. Have you ever made a dessert? What is your favourite sweet treat?

Written by Gill Munton

Vocabulary check

Discuss the meaning (as used in the non-fiction text) after the children have read the word.

	definition
feast	*a wonderful meal*
carton	*a box*
dairy cream	*the thick part of milk*
steps	*things to do*
scoops	*big spoonfuls*
pips	*the small hard seeds in fruit*

Punctuation to note:

Read Make	
	Capital letters that start sentences
.	*Full stop at the end of each sentence*
!	*Exclamation marks to show that something is suprising or exciting*
'	*Apostrophe to show something is missing. In* it's *'i' is missing and* it's *really means* it is
:	*A colon to show that a list of things is going to follow*

Read this book and see how you can make a peach treat.

It's cheap to make and it's a real feast!

Make lots of peach treats for your next birthday party!

You need:

- some cake
- a carton of custard
- a can of dairy cream
- some grapes
- a tin of sweet peaches
- a chocolate flake.

Now follow the 7 easy steps.

1 First, take a chunk of cake. Put it in a clean glass bowl.

This will make the base of your peach treat.

2 Now take 4 scoops of custard.
Put the custard on top of the cake.

3 Put a big blob
of dairy cream
on top of the
custard.

4 Take the pips out of the grapes and put the grapes on top of the cream.

5 Chop up the peach and put the bits on top of the cream with the grapes. Heap them up.

Ask an adult to help you with opening the tin of peaches and with cutting.

6 Finish off the peach treat by sticking a chocolate flake in the cream.

7 Now take your seat for a real treat!

Eat it with a spoon.

Peach treats are so cool!

Questions to talk about

Re-read the page. Read the question to the children. Tell them whether it is a FIND IT *question
or* PROVE IT *question.*

FIND IT	PROVE IT
✓ Turn to the page	✓ Turn to the page
✓ Read the question	✓ Read the question
✓ Find the answer	✓ Find your evidence
	✓ Explain why

Page 10:	FIND IT	*How many chocolate flakes do you need to make a peach treat?*
Page 11:	FIND IT	*How many steps does it take to make a peach treat?*
Page 11:	FIND IT	*What sort of bowl do you need?*
Page 14:	PROVE IT	*What do you need a knife for?*
Page 16:	FIND IT	*What do you use to eat a peach treat?*
Page 16:	PROVE IT	*Do you think the child likes peach treats? Why/Why not?*

Questions to read and answer ✴ ✴

(Children complete without your help.)

1 What treat does this book show you?

2 What goes on top of the custard?

3 Why do you think you take the pips out of the grapes?

4 What goes on top of the cream?

5 Why do you think you need an adult to help?